AF498400

Indian Rights and Our Duties

LIBRARY OF CONGRESS

LIBRARY OF CONG. LIBRARY OF CONG. LIBRARY OF CONG. LIBRARY OF CONG. LIBRARY OF

[illegible]

ADDRESS

[illegible]

DELIVERED AT

[illegible]

[illegible]

LIBRARY OF CONGRESS

INDIAN RIGHTS

AND

OUR DUTIES.

AN

ADDRESS

DELIVERED AT

IHERST, HARTFORD, ETC.

DECEMBER, 1829.

BY HEMAN HUMPHREY, D. D.
'President of Amherst College.

Price Two Cents.

ereotyped for the Association for diffusing information on the subject of
Indian Rights.

1831.

E93
H923

What the Indians have most to lament for the past and to fear for the future is, the apathy of their friends. Could these be roused up to do what is in their power—first, to inform the public mind, and second, to effect an expression of *public opinion*, by petitions to Congress, they would have little to fear from their enemies. It is a *fact*, and one that ought to be known, that Christians have been deterred from the public expression of their opinions and feelings in favor of the Indians, by a fear of the imputation of political motives. But should not the language of every Christian, and every man of humanity, be—*Whilst I will not be influenced by party politics to espouse the cause of the Indians, neither will I be prevented from doing my duty to them, by the charge of being actuated by that motive.*

The Minister to whom this is sent, is solicited to procure, or get some *member of his church* to procure a small contribution, to purchase (at two cents a-piece) one copy for every family in his congregation; to send to Albany for them; and when received, to have them distributed without delay.

Should there be in his place of residence, any other minister of any denomination, who may not have received a copy, he is requested to endeavor to get him to do the same in his congregation.

☞ Orders to be sent to Ebenezer Watson, Albany.

☞ Any parcels wanted for the *southern* or *eastern states*, he wil have immediately *dispatched from New-York*, where the work i printed. Particular directions *should be given as to the mode* of foi warding them.

ADDRESS.

The people of the land have used oppression, and exercised robbery, and have vexed the poor and needy; yea, they have oppressed the stranger wrongfully. And I sought for a man among them that should make up the hedge, and stand in the gap before me for the land, that I should not destroy it: but I found none. Therefore have I poured out mine indignation upon them; I have consumed them with the fire of my wrath; their own way have I recompensed upon their heads, saith the Lord God.—
EZEKIEL.

ABOUT nine hundred years before this appalling record was made by the prophet, God denounced against Israel the very punishment which is here declared to have been inflicted. This denunciation was communicated to the people by their great law-giver, at the foot of Mount Sinai. "Thou shalt neither vex a stranger nor oppress him; for ye were strangers in the land of Egypt. Ye shall not afflict any widow or fatherless child: if thou afflict them in any wise and they cry at all unto me, I will surely hear their cry; and my wrath shall wax hot, and I will kill you with the sword, and your wives shall be widows and your children fatherless."

How long the Israelites remembered their own sufferings in Egypt, and were restrained from deeds of violence and oppression, we are not informed. But we learn from Ezekiel, that regardless of justice and humanity, and in defiance of the wrath of God revealed from heaven, they at length used oppression and exercised robbery, and vexed the poor and needy, and oppressed the stranger wrongfully. And though the prophets and some few others boldly remonstrated, though they exhorted the people to repent, and would fain have averted the threatened judgments by their prayers, they were borne down and disheartened by the overwhelming torrent of corruption. No man in authority was found to second their efforts. Neither the king, nor any of his nobles or counsellors stood in the gap. None of them employed their abilities and influence to stop the progress of wickedness and rescue those who were crying to God from under the hand of violence; wherefore, he poured out his fury upon the people and consumed them with the fire of his anger.

And is there no monitory voice addressed to other nations in all this? Or if there be, are we at liberty to place it on the same ground with other ancient historical records? Wo to the politician, wo to the moralist, who shall attempt thus to bring down the writings of Moses and the prophets to a level with Josephus and Tacitus. If the historical and prophetical books of the Old Testament are true, they are inspired, and, as an apostle assures us "are profitable for doctrine, for reproof, for correction, for instruction, in righteousness."

And perhaps of all nations, whether ancient or modern, we are most deeply interested in the dealings of God with the children of Israel. In looking back upon their deliverances and their sins, most emphatically may we repeat and appropriate to ourselves the words of Paul to the Corinthians; "Now all these things happened unto them for ensamples, and they are written for our admonition, upon whom the ends of the world are come."

Are we then of these United States chargeable with violence, oppression, and robbery? Is the unoffending and beseeching stranger any where vexed and persecuted in this boasted land of religion, justice, and humanity? Is there an individual, is there a whole people at the present moment, either suffering from our rapacity, or trembling at our cruel menaces? Would God that we could indignantly answer these questions in the negative. Would God that the recorded testimony of our intentional encroachments upon the sacred rights of humanity could be prevented from crossing the ocean in every ship, to excite the loud derision of all the enemies of republican institutions.

I allude not here to African servitude. For terrible as it is over one half the land, it is a hereditary curse and shame, against which the constituted authorities of the nation, in obedience to the voice of the people, long since bore their solemn testimony by prohibiting the importation of slaves.

But there is another, and a still more interesting people, dwelling within the limits of what we have been pleased to mark off as our national territory, who have already been subjected, I had almost said, to a harder fate than the Africans themselves. The first European settlers found them here, the immemorial possessors and undisputed lords of the country; and what has become of those powerful tribes that two centuries ago dwelt where we now dwell; and kindled their watch-fires where our proudest cities stand; and owned all these rivers, and bays, and harbors, and great lakes, and lofty mountains and fertile vallies? Where are they? A nobler race of wild men never existed in any age or country. We are accustomed to speak of them as ferocious savages.— And it is true they were uncivilized. They had no schools nor Colleges. They had never enjoyed the blessed light of Christianity; and in their wars with one another they were as cruel as they were brave and crafty. It is true, also, that when we began to extend our settlements far into the country, and they saw us in possession of their finest hunting grounds and fisheries, they became jealous of us, and being instigated by our enemies, the French, who then flanked our whole northern and western frontier, from the gulph of St. Lawrence to the mouth of the Missouri, they made depredations upon our property, and cruelly butchered some of our people.

All this is true. But savages as they were, they bore with our gradual encroachments much longer than we should have done with theirs under similar circumstances, and taught us lessons which may well put to the blush all our boasted religion and civilization.

"The Indians," says Dr. Trumbull, "at the first settlement of our fathers, performed many acts of kindness toward them. They instructed them in the manner of planting and dressing the Indian corn. They carried them safe through rivers and waters. They gave them much useful information respecting the country, and when the English and their children were lost in the woods, and were in danger of perishing with hunger or cold, they conducted them to their wigwams, fed them and restored them to their families and parents. By selling them corn when pinched with famine, they relieved their distresses and prevented their perishing in a strange land and uncultivated wilderness." The same historian tells us, "that it was nearly sixteen years after the settlement of Plymouth, before the Indians commenced hostilities upon their English neighbors:" and again, "that the English lived in tolerable peace with all the Indians in New-England, except the Pequots, for about forty years."

Thus, when we were few and they were many; we were weak and they were strong—instead of driving us back into the sea, as they might have done at any time, they cherished our perilous infancy, and tendered to us the sacred emblems of peace. They gave us land, as much as we wanted, or sold it to us for nothing. They permitted us quietly to clear up the wilderness, and to build habitations, and school houses, and churches. And when every thing began to smile around us, under the combined influence of industry, education, and religion, these savages did not come to us and say, "We want your houses—we want your fine cultivated farms—you must move off. There is room enough for you beyond the western rivers, where you may settle down on a better soil, and begin anew."

Nor, because we were strongly attached to our firesides and to our fathers' sepulchres, did they say, " You are mere tenants at will : we own all the land, and if you insist upon staying longer you must dissolve your government and submit to such laws as we choose to make for you."

No—the Indian tribes of the seventeenth century knew nothing of these modern refinements : they were no such adepts in the law of nature and of nations. They allowed us to abide by our own council fires, and to govern ourselves as we chose, when they could either have dispossessed or subjugated us at pleasure We *did* remain, and we gradually waxed rich and strong. We wanted more land, and they sold it to us at our own price. Still we are not satisfied. There was room enough to the west, and we advised them to move farther back. If they took our advice, well. If not, we knew how to enforce it. And where are those once terrible nations now? Driven alternately by purchase and by conquest, from river to river, and from mountain to mountain, they have disappeared with their own gigantic forests, and we, their enlightened heirs at law and the sword, now plough up their bones with as much indifference as we do their arrows. Shall I name the Mohegans, the Pequots, the Iroquois, and the Mohawks? What has become of them, and of a hundred other independent nations which dwelt on this side of the Mississippi when we landed at Plymouth and at James' Town? Here and there, as at Penobscot, and Mashpee, and Oneida, you may see a diminutive and downcast remnant, wandering like troubled ghosts among the graves of their mighty progenitors. Thus have our trinkets, our threats, our arms, our whiskey, our bribes, and our vices, all but annihilated those vast physical and intellectual energies of a native population, which for more than a hundred and fifty years could make us quake and flee at pleasure throughout all our northern, western, and southern borders.

There is something more than metaphor, more than the wild flowers of Indian rhetoric, in the speech of a distinguished chief to General Knox, about the close of the last century. "Brother, I have been looking at your beautiful city—the great waters—your fine country, and I see how you all are. But then I could not help thinking that this fine country, and this great water, were once ours. Our ancestors lived here; they enjoyed it as their own place; it was the gift of the Great Spirit to them and their children. At last the white people came here in a great canoe. They asked us only to let them tie it to a tree, lest the waters should carry it away; we consented. They said some of their people were sick, and asked leave to land them and put them under the shade of the trees. The ice then came, and they could not go away. They begged for a piece of land to build wigwams for the winter; we granted it to them. Then they asked for some corn to keep them from starving; and we kindly furnished it to them.

"Afterward more came. They brought spirituous and intoxicating liquors with them, of which the Indians were very fond. They persuaded us to sell them some land. Finally they drove us back from time to time, into the wilderness, far from the water and the fishes. They have destroyed the game; and our people have wasted away;

and now we live miserable and wretched, while you are·enjoying our fine and beautiful country. This makes me sorry, brother, and I cannot help it."

Here is truth and nature; nor is there less of either in the speech of the famous Logan to Lord Dunmore, governor of Virginia.

"My cabin, since I had one of my own, has ever been open to any white man who wanted shelter. My spoils of hunting, since first I began to range these woods, have I ever imparted to appease his hunger, to clothe his nakedness. But what have I seen? What! But that at my return at night, laden with spoil, my numerous family lie bleeding on the ground by the hand of those who had found my little hut a certain refuge from the storm, who had eaten my food, who had covered themselves with my skins. What have I seen? What! But that those dear little mouths for which I had all day toiled, when I returned to fill them, had not one word to thank me for all that toil.

"What could I resolve upon! My blood boiled within me. My heart leaped to my mouth! Nevertheless, I bid my tomahawk be quiet, and lie at rest, for that war, because I thought the great men of your country sent them not to do it. Not long after, some of your men invited our tribe to cross the river and bring their venison with them. They came as they had been invited. The white men then made them drunk, murdered them, and turned their knives even against the women. Was not my own sister among them? Was she not scalped by the hands of the very man whom she had taught to escape his enemies when they were scenting out his track? What could I resolve upon? My blood boiled thrice hotter than before. Thrice again my heart leaped to my mouth. I bade no longer my tomahawk to be quiet and rest for that war.

"I sprang from my cabin to avenge their blood, and fully have I done it in this war, by shedding yours, from your coldest to your hottest sun. I am now for peace—to peace have I advised most of my countrymen. Nay, what is more, I have offered, I will offer myself a victim, being ready to die if their good requires it. Think not that I fear death. I have no relatives left to mourn for me. Logan's blood runs in no veins but these. I would not turn my heel to save my life, and why should I? For I have neither wife, nor child, nor sister, to howl for me when I am gone!"

Gone is the mighty warrior, the terrible avenger, the heart-bursting orator. Gone is the terror and glory of his nation; and gone for ever from our elder states, are the red men, who, like Saul and Jonathan, were "swifter than eagles, and stronger than lions;" and who, with the light and advantages which we enjoy, might have rivalled us in wealth and power—in the senate and the forum—as I am sure they would have surpassed us in. magnanimity and justice.

But while the besom of destruction has thus swept away more than nine tenths of the aboriginal sovereignties of the country, a few of the more southern tribes have hitherto in a measure escaped, though greatly reduced both in numbers and territory. And where is the philanthropist who has not rejoiced to see these tribes emerging so rapidly from Pagan darkness, and coming into the light of well regulated, civil and Christian communities? How delightful has it been to dwell on the hope that the Cherokees, the Choctaws, and their aboriginal neighbors, on this side the great river of the west, would be permitted to make their new and glorious experiment upon the soil which God gave to their fathers. What bright visions of their future intellectual and moral elevation have shed the glories of a new creation upon all their mountains and plains!

But what cloud is that which now darkens their heavens? What voices of supplication and wo are heard from all their dwellings? The crisis of their fate has suddenly come. The decree has gone forth. The most unjust and oppressive measures are in train, either to drive 70,000 unoffending people from the soil on which they were born, into distant wilds, where most of them will perish, or to dissolve their respective independent governments, rob them of their lands and bring them under strange laws, the very design of which is to break down their national spirit, and insure their speedy extermination.

To go fully into the great question of Indian rights,

which is now pending before the American people, and
which ought to rouse up all the holy sympathies of humanity, justice, and religion in the land, would require a
volume ; but the facts in the case, on which the verdict
of all generations must rest, may be stated in a few words.

And here, let every friend to his country enter his solemn protest against any attempt which may be made
to bring down this great question to the sordid level of
party politics.   Nothing can be more preposterous, nothing more unsafe.   We are all interested in giving the
Indians a fair hearing, and in taking care that no injustice
be done them.   All parties have a common interest in
preserving the faith and honor of the nation, whoever
may happen for the time to administer the government.

What then are the facts in the case before us—facts
which it is impossible to dispute, without first burning up
the records at Washington?   What are the rights of the
Cherokees, and of the other tribes within the chartered limits of Georgia, Alabama, and Mississippi?   What is
their present condition?   What are the evils which now
threaten them?   And what is the course which the general government is solemnly bound to pursue in this
emergency.

The Indian tribes then, whose fate at this moment
hangs in awful suspense, are, and always have been distinct national sovereignties.   In their present location
they have all the rights of preoccupancy.   The first white
settlers found them in the undisputed possession of the
wilderness which they are now so fast turning into a
fruitful field—and of much larger and more fertile terri-
tories which they have since ceded to the United States.
The land was theirs by the highest possible title.   The
Creator and proprietor of all lands gave it to them.   It
has the Indian title now in question ever been recogniz-
ed as valid by the United States' government?   Always
Has the right of these tribes to govern themselves, and
exercise the prerogatives of independent states ever been
called in question?   Never, till very lately.   On these
points there is no room left for debate.   Our government
has always treated them as bodies politic, enjoying no
merely the right of occupancy, but of absolute property
and self control on their respective reservation.

Solemn treaties have been made with them, by all our Presidents, and sanctioned, as the constitution directs, by the Senate, with all the formalities of its high prerogative. In every one of these treaties the faith of the nation is pledged; and I bless God that hitherto that faith has never been violated. Such is the solemn, and cruel mockery, (if the treaties be not binding,) by which the Cherokees, and other tribes at the south, have been induced to make, cession after cession, to the United States, till more than three-fourths of their original territory, including nearly all the most fertile tracts, are in our hands. And they indulged the hope, no doubt, that a magnanimous people would at last be satisfied to leave them their sterile mountains, and few remaining vallies, without importunity—certainly without violent seizure. But in this, alas, they find themselves grievously disappointed. Give, give, is the cry which continues to vex their ears and sadden their hearts.

They are now distinctly told, "You can no longer be tolerated as distinct communities here. A sovereign and independent state cannot permit the existence of other sovereignties within its limits. We want your lands, and we are determined to have them. You must set your faces, with your wives and children, toward the Rocky Mountains, and settle down where you will have more room, and be better off than here. Do you say you will not go? Then stay and take the consequences. We shall on make you repent of your obstinacy. Put out your council fires—demolish your court-houses—burn up your laws—depose your chiefs—and come under our jurisdiction—not to enjoy equal rights with ourselves, but to be degraded and treated as incorrigible savages." This is the alternative which is now presented to 70,000 men, women, and children, in the 19th century, and under the sanction of the most enlightened and Christian republic on earth. O tell it not in Gath! If such a construction of the most solemn treaties, and guarantees is to prevail; if the faith of this great nation is thus to be given to the four winds, then let me plead for the Indians while I may— for who can tell how long he shall be permitted to enjoy this, or any other constitutional right?

But why are the Choctaws and Cherokees so unwilling

to remove? What is their present condition? And what are the prospects which are opening upon them, if permitted to remain where they are? Full answers to these questions would require hours, instead of a few moments. The truth is, that a mighty change is taking place in the character and condition of the southern Indians. Under the influence of industrious habits, of education, of religion, and of efficient laws, they are waking up to a new existence. It may be doubted whether civilization ever advanced more rapidly in any part of the world than it is now advancing in some of their districts. Having abandoned the chase, multitudes of them are living in the enjoyment of independence and plenty, in comfortable houses, and upon their own well cultivated farms. They wear their own domestic fabricks. They have their mills, their mechanics, their labor-saving machinery, their schools, and their own Cadmus, too, under whose instruction, a nation may almost literally learn to read in a day. They have, too, their legislative assemblies; their courts of civil and criminal jurisdiction; their juries; and nearly all the safe-guards of life, liberty, and property, which exist in the best regulated communities. For the suppression of intemperance, gaming, and other kindred vices, it may safely be affirmed, that they have as good laws as any of their English neighbors, and they execute them at least as well. To give a single example: "A case occurred in the Cherokee nation last spring, where one of the judges of the circuit court, on finding the air of the court-house strongly impregnated with whiskey, ordered the sheriff to follow certain suspected persons to their haunts in the woods, where he found and poured out the contraband article before their eyes. By the same judge, six men were fined fifty dollars each, for gambling, and one was fined for profane swearing." Add to all this, the Christian religion is taking deep root and rapidly filling the wilderness with churches and songs of salvation, under the instructions of pious teachers, and the remarkable effusion of the Holy Spirit.

Now, in view of all these circumstances and brightening prospects, can it be wondered at that the Indians are unwilling to remove? And who that has a home of his own, and a heart of flesh in his bosom, can wish them to go, contrary to their will ? Who that is not dead to sympathy, and deaf to justice, can resist the imploring appeal, which was lately made by a Choctaw chief, to the agent of our government ? I wish a copy of it could be placed in every dwelling in the land, and read every evening, in every domestic circle, till every child should learn it by heart.

"We do not wish to sell our land and remove. This land our great Father above gave us. We stand on it. We stood on it before the white man came to the edge of the American land. It belongs to no one in any place but ourselves. Our land is not borrowed land. White men came and sat down here and there all round us. When they wished to buy land of us we have had good counsels together. The white man always said the land is *yours*, it is *yours*." Poor simple souls ! these savages thought the white men meant as they said, and would do as they promised !

"We have always been true friends to the American people. We have not spoiled the least thing belonging to an American. But now we are told, that the king of Mississippi is about to extend his laws over us. We, the chiefs and beloved men in this nation, are distressed. Our hands are not strong ; we are a small people ; we do not know much. We are distressed. Colonel Ward knows that we have just begun to build new houses, and make new fields, and purchase iron. We have begun to make axes, hoes and ploughs. We have some schools. We have begun to learn, and we have also begun to embrace the gospel.

"We are like an infant that has just begun to walk ; we have just begun to rise and go. And now our great father, who sits in the white house looking this way, says to us : 'Unless you go yonder, the white man will extend his laws over you.' We do not say that his words are lies, but we are distressed. Oh that our great father would love us ! O that the king of Mississippi would love us ! The American people say they love liberty : they talk much about it. They boast of their own liberty. Why will they take it from the red men ?"

Take it from the red men ! With our consent, shall either the lands, or the liberty of these red men ever be taken from them ? Never ! What ! either drive them into the great western desert ; then over the Rocky Mountains ; and finally into the Pacific Ocean ; or else dissolve their governments, and crush them where they are ! God forbid that such inhumanity, that such injustice should ever stain the pages of our history. I had almost said, that such a record shall not go down to posterity. But, how can I hinder it? I am but an humble individual. I can have but little influence any where, and none where influence is most needed. But, as yet, I am free. I bless God, that I have a heart which cannot help being distressed for the poor persecuted Indians. I have a voice, feeble though it be, and no man, without the scimitar or bow string, shall hinder my pleading for the oppressed. I have a right to petition, to remonstrate, to implore, and God forbid that I should be silent. It shall be my aim, and my glory, at this fearful crisis, to enlist as many hearts, and tongues, and pens, and prayers as possible in the sacred cause of humanity, of national faith, and of eternal justice. I had rather receive the blessing of one poor Cherokee. as he casts his last look back upon his country, for having, though in vain, attempted to prevent his being driven from it, than to sleep beneath the marble of all the Cæsars.

Shall "I be told that all this is idle preaching"—that I have entirely mistaken the policy of Georgia in reference to the Cherokees—that she has no thoughts of compelling tham to emigrate? I am astonished that such an expedient should be resorted to, to quiet the friends of the Indians, and to ward off public remonstrance. It is an insult offered to the common sense of the nation. What? Tell the Indians, "We want your country, and you had better leave it—You can never be quiet and happy here?" And then, because they do not take your advice, cut it up into counties, declare all their laws and usages, after a certain day, to be null and void, and substitute laws which it is known they cannot live under ; and then turn round and coolly tell the world, "Oh ! we mean no compulsion ! The fartherest in the world from it ! If these people choose to stay, why by all means let them remain where they are." These are the tender mercies of which we shall undoubtedly learn more in due time.   And it all amounts to this.   "You have got a fine farm and I want it.   It makes a notch in a corner of mine.   I will help you to move *five hundred* miles into the wilderness, and there give you more and better land, which you may cultivate and enjoy without molestation "as long as grass grows and water runs."* You *must* go:—however, do just as you please.   I shall never resort to any other compulsion than just to lay you under certain necessary restrictions.   Perhaps, for instance, as I am the strongest, and you have more land than you want, I may take two thirds, or three fourths of it from you; but then there shall be no *compulsion!*   Stay upon what is left if you choose.   I may also find it necessary to ask you for your house, and if you should not give it up, I may be driven to the disagreeable necessity of chaining you to a ring bolt and giving you a few salutary stripes —not to *compel* you to flee from your habitation the moment you can get loose, (for compulsion, of all things, I abhor,) but just to induce you to emigrate *willingly*."

This my friends is the kind of *free agency* taught in the new school of metaphysics, which the Indians must learn and exercise whether they will or not—but as no such school is yet established in this part of the land, we must be excused in adhering, for the present, to our old fashioned notions about free agency, public faith, and common bounty.

I maintain, then, that it is the bounden duty of the general Government to protect the Indians, not only in the enjoyment of their country, but of their laws.   If it is possible for treaties to bind a nation in any case, then are we bound.   If there is any such thing as public faith, then is ours solemnly pledged to a single Tribe nearly twenty times over.   If that pile of Indian treaties, now in the office of State, is any thing more than a pile of frauds and insults, then the Government must interpose its strong arm to prevent aggression.   Take the following as specimens of these compacts.   Treaty of Holliston, Art. 7.   "The United States solemnly guarantee to the Cherokee nation all their lands not hitherto ceded."

Treaty of Tellico, Art. 6.   "The United States will

* Query—How long does *water run* in the region destined for the future residence of the Indians?

continue the guarantee of theirs, that is, the Cherokee
country, FOREVER, as made and contained in former treaties."   And who, let me ask, will stop to inquire, at this
early period, when the first jubilee of our independence
is hardly past, whether our most solemn national pledges
shall be redeemed?   I feel confident that all the charges
which can be rung upon state rights, and that terrific
phrase, *imperium in imperio,* to drive the Indians from
their country, will never satisfy the American people.
The very summary process of disinheriting 70,000 persons at once by a novel construction of the Constitution,
which begs the whole question—will never be sanctioned
in the council of *twelve millions.* I repeat it—our government must defend the Indians against all encroachments and usurpations whatsoever, or stand before the
world convicted of a disregard to public faith which it
makes one shudder to think of.

Under these circumstances, who can doubt, that if the
voice of the whole American people could be heard in
the Capitol to-morrow, a great majority of them would
implore and conjure both houses of Congress to interpose
and save the character of the nation?   And if I am not
mistaken in this supposition, it is still possible to avert
the ruin which is now impending over the Cherokees and
their red brethren at the south.   It is indeed the eleventh
hour; but they *can* be saved.   The sovereignty of this
great nation resides in the people; and what should hinder them from speaking in the ears of our rulers, "like
the voice of many waters?"   Let them speak, and the
thing is done.   The Indians can be saved with infinite-
ly less expense of time and trouble than it costs every
four years, to decide whether A or B or C shall be our
next President.

But perhaps some will despairingly ask, "What can
we do here, in one corner of the land?"   What can *we*
do? We shall never know till WE TRY.   Injustice and
cruelty have carried the day a thousand times through
the mere apathy and discouragements of those who might
have triumphed like Sampson.   I will mention some things
which we can do.   We can *feel* for the persecuted remnant of that noble race of men upon whose soil we are
building up a great empire.   We can commune together

respecting their wrongs, and the dangers which surround them, till "our hearts burn within us." We can contribute in various ways, to lay the facts on which the justice of their cause rests, before such of our fellow-citizens as may not have had access to these facts. We can send in our petitions to Congress, and we can induce others to do the same. In the mean time, it cannot be doubted that the friends of justice and humanity will be active in almost every section of the country. Thus we may hope that there will be a general and simultaneous movement of the people toward Washington.

And in this view of the case, will any one still demand "Who are we, and what are our numbers, that we should hope to gain a hearing in the high places of power?" I answer, we are, what our public servants delight to call us, *the sovereign people*—we are *all* the people, and that is enough. Every man in the nation, however poor, can go to Washington upon this business for nothing, as fast as the wheels of government can carry him. You understand perfectly what I mean. We can all be heard in the Senate house by our petitions, if we please. We can block up the avenues which lead to it, with the multitude of our signatures; and whatever measures the voice of the nation shall demand, will ultimately be taken.

Above all, we can send up our united petitions to the Court of Heaven, where the cause of the poor and the oppressed is never disregarded. And if the sublime experiment which the southern tribes of Indians are making, of civilization and self-government, should fail, through the cruel interference of white men, it is my solemn conviction that it will be owing to the criminal supineness of those who in heart and conscience are opposed to such interference. For I will not believe, I cannot believe, that the coveters of other men's vineyards, and their abettors in this land, are more than a lean minority of the whole people. If our government was despotic the case would be different. We should not be answerable for measures over which we could exercise no control. But. living as we do, under rulers of our own choice, we are answerable if we neglect to exert our influence to the utmost in favor of righteousness, humanity, and public faith.

But suppose the worst—suppose the government should

turn a deaf ear to our remonstrances.   Let us not forget
that *duties* are ours, while *events* belong to God.   If we
do what we can to save the Indians in this hour of their
anguish and jeopardy, their blood will not be found in
our skirts, though they should be trodden into the graves
of their fathers, or be driven away to perish in deserts
so remote that the "ill savor" of their carcasses may not
come up into the nostrils of their destroyers.

Do we then want motives for action at this critical,
this awful juncture?   Such a crisis does not happen once
in a century.   Nothing like it is to be found in the history of our country hitherto, and I pray God that no
such crisis may ever occur here again.   War has rava-
ged the land more than once, or twice, with its tempests
of fire and blood; but the question was never agitated
till now, whether the public faith is to be held sacred or
not.   Who would have dared in the days of Washington,
or Jefferson, to have broached such doctrines as have re-
cently been promulgated by the highest authority in the
nation?   How long ago, think you, could any man have
gained a hearing to arguments which, if admitted, go to
annihilate the faith of all our treaties?

I repeat the assertion, that we have come to such a
crisis as neither we nor our fathers ever saw before.

The great question is to be finally settled within a few
months, perhaps weeks, whether whole, peaceable nations
shall be dispossessed, or virtually enslaved, under the eye,
and with the approbation of a government which is solemnly pledged to protect them.   And do we want motives to remonstrate against this crying injustice?   Really,
the motives are so many and so urgent—they throng so
importunately about my path, that I know not what to
do with them.   Thrusting the greater part of them aside,
I can only bestow a few moments upon some of the most
prominent.

And the *first* motive is drawn from the immutable and
eternal principles of humanity and justice.   Humanity
pleads for the Indians with all her inexhaustable sympathies, and with all her eloquent tongues.   They are distressed.   They are vexed.   They are persecuted.   The
bosoms of tens of thousands of unoffending people are
heaving with a common and mighty agony—occasioned

by the encroachments and menaces of those who ought
to be their protectors.   And where, if we do not speak
and act, is our humanity.

Justice too, with all its irrefragable arguments, urges
us to remonstrate and to act.   The most sacred rights of
four nations, living under our protection and confiding
in our republican faith, are invaded.   And they cry to us
for help.   The heritage which God gave them is to be
wrested from them; or if permitted to retain the small
portion of it which is now under cultivation, they are to
be thrust down from their moral and political elevation,
into the depths of despondency and ruin.   And can any
one who knows all this sit still and be quiet.

What if only ten poor families in a remote corner of
Maine or Missouri were threatened with similar outrage?
Every man in the nation would rise up and blow the
trumpet with all his might.   What if some lordly op-
pressor, having already ten times as much land as he
could cultivate, should go to these families and say, " You
must move off.   I want your little farms, and will not
take a denial "—Ten millions of voices would answer in
thunder, " *You sha'nt have them!*   No, never!   These
families have rights as well as you, and they shall be
protected at all hazards."   And where, I ask, is the difference?   In the case supposed there are *ten* families, and
in that of the Indians now under consideration, there are
ten or fifteen thousand!   Where is the difference?   Ah,
the ten are *white* men, and the *ten thousand* are *red* men!
Where is the difference?   The former are protected in
their rights by the constitution, and the latter by the solemn faith of treaties!—there is the mighty difference!!

A *second* motive, then, for stirring up all the moral
power of this nation at this time, is found in the danger
which threatens our own liberties.   This suggestion, I
am aware, will be ridiculed by many, and regarded by
most as the offspring of a terrified imagination.   Let
those who choose, cry, "Peace and safety," and fold
their arms and wait for the march of events.   But if the
people sit still, and look calmly on, while the Indians are
abandoned to their fate, in violation of the most solemn
compacts, what security have we that the same government which deliberately breaks its treaties in the face of

heaven and earth, will not, ten, or twenty years hence, find some plausible pretext for turning its power and patronage against the constitution itself? And if it should, how long, think you, will these paper and parchment bulwarks of ours stand? How long will it be a blessing to be born and live in America, rather than in Turkey, or under the Autocrat of all the Russians?

Do you tell me that there is no possible danger—that no man, or number of men, will ever dare to assail our free and glorious institutions. Let the history of republics, or rather let their tombstones decide this point between us. So it would have been said when Washington and Jefferson were at the head of our affairs, that nobody would ever dare to disinherit, or enslave the Indians, protected as they are by almost a hundred and fifty treaties. And yet it is about to be done. And how much better is our parchment than theirs? If such encroachments, acquiesced in, do not prepare the way for putting shackles upon our children, they must be protected by higher munitions than constitutional bulwarks. This I am willing to leave upon record, and run the risk of its being laughed at fifty years hence.

A *third* motive for earnest remonstrance at the present crisis, is found in the grand experiment which we as a nation are now making, before the whole world, of the superior excellence and stability of republican institutions. How many thousand times has the parallel been proudly drawn by our statesmen and orators, between this country and every other nation under heaven. How triumphantly has it been proclaimed in the ears of all mankind, that here, at least, all the rights of the weak as well as the strong have found a sure protection. But let the stroke which is now impending, fall upon the heads of the poor defenceless Indians, and who will not be heartily and forever ashamed of all this boasting? Who will ever dare to say another word about the partition of Poland? Who in a foreign land will ever hereafter be willing to own that he is an American. How will all the enlightened friends of free institutions in other countries mourn over this indelible stigma upon our national character; and how will the enemies of equal rights triumph in our disgrace. Verily, "we are made a spectacle to the world, and to angels, and to men."

The *last* motive which I have time to mention, and can but just allude to, is, that there is a just God in heaven, and that sooner or later his wrath will wax hot against the nation that tramples upon the rights of its defenceless and imploring neighbors. Tell me not of your twelve millions of people—of the exploits of your armies and navy—of the unparalleled growth and inexhaustible resources of the country. What will all these avail when God shall come out of his place to "make inquisition for blood?" Prouder and mightier nations than this have fallen, and how can we expect to escape if we "use oppression, and exercise robbery, and vex the poor and needy?"

The Cherokees and Choctaws cannot, indeed, resist our arms. They lie at the mercy of their white neighbors. They are like little trembling flocks of kids, surrounded by lions. But though they are too weak to meet us in the field, they are not too weak to lift up their cries to heaven against us. Though they are too few to defend their country against our rapacity, there are enough of them to "appear as swift witnesses against us" in the Court above? and they will assuredly have the right of testifying secured to them there, however they may be restricted and oppressed in courts below. Their numbers are more than sufficient to bring down the judgments of God upon their cruel oppressors. Who then will "make up the hedge, and stand in the gap before Him for the land that He should not destroy it?" The crisis is awful, and the responsibilities of our rulers and of the whole nation is tremendous! The Lord is a holy God, and he is jealous!

[*See next page.*

At a meeting of gentlemen from all parts of the Commonwealth, in the hall of the House of Representatives, *Boston*, February 8, 1830,* a Memorial to Congress was presented, and after having been read, its adoption was moved by Mr. CHOATE, and seconded by Mr. SALTONSTALL. Both these gentlemen made able and conclusive speeches, in support of the perfect right of the Indians to the lands which they occupy. The Memorial was unanimously adopted; and the Chairman and Secretaries were requested to sign it in behalf of the meeting, and to forward it to Congress. Here follows the Memorial.

Mr. WORCESTER then moved the following resolutions:

Resolved, That the pending controversy, in regard to the rights of the Indians, is a subject which eminently calls for the expression of public opinion; and that we therefore strongly recommend to our fellow citizens, that public meetings be held, resolutions adopted, and memorials forwarded, by the friends of justice and of our national honor, in every part of the United States.

Resolved, That since the Indians must look to the interposition of Congress, as the only probable way in which their rights can be defended, it is important that members of our National Legislature should be aware of the deep interest which is felt in this subject by a very large portion of their constituents; and that there is far more danger of apathy and indifference, when our national character for good faith and fair dealing is in question, than of too much zeal and earnestness in behalf of the hitherto unsullied honor of our country, or of too much sympathy with the weak and suffering.

The mover supported the resolutions in a short speech, the purport of which was, that if the cause of the Indians is lost, it will be lost by the indifference, the apathy, the criminal negligence of the people of the United States.

The resolutions were seconded by HENRY SHAW, Esq. of Lanesborough, who warmly approved of the manner in which the meeting had been conducted; namely, by addressing the reason and judgment, by regular legal and constitutional arguments. He also decidedly approved the assembling of the people, in orderly meetings, to consider questions of this kind.

The Committee were then directed to publish the Memorial, and to address a Circular Letter to their fellow citizens in every part of the Commonwealth.

Every question was carried without a dissenting voice.

Both the meetings were highly respectable, on account of the number and the character of gentlemen who were present.

* See page 2 of the cover.

RD 1 2.8   MB

CIRCULAR LETTER.

FELLOW CITIZENS,   Boston, February 1830.

At a very respectable meeting of gentlemen from all parts of the Commonwealth, convened by public notice in the Hall of the House of Representatives of the State House in Boston, on the 21st ult., the undersigned were appointed a Committee of Correspondence; and it was made one part of their duty to address a Circular Letter, on the present relations between the United States and the Indians, to their fellow citizens in all parts of the Commonwealth.

When the foregoing Memorial was adopted, which was on the 8th inst., at a very respectable meeting, of which public notice had also been given, the same duty was again assigned to the Committee; and, in both instances, the assignment was made without a dissenting voice.

The Committee are impelled, therefore, by the instructions of the meeting, as well as by their own feelings, to address a few words to the friends of humanity and justice in every part of the Commonwealth, on this exceedingly important subject.

The question now depending, as it is understood by multitudes of candid and intelligent men, in nearly all parts of the United States, is no less than this *Shall the people of the United States faithfully observe the solemn treaties which they have made with the Cherokees and other Indian nations—according to the true intent and meaning of those engagements, and the understanding of the parties?*

You will exclaim at once, *It is impossible that there should be any doubt how this question must be answered.* We would gladly think so too; but when we call to mind that some politicians gravely declare Indian communities *not to be nations*, and treaties with Indians *not to be binding;* and that other politicians insist on *expediency*, as the only proper rule of public morality, so far as Indians are concerned; when we find some writers and speakers refuse to look at public engagements with the Indians, but plead the right of releasing themselves from these engagements on the ground that Indians are poor, and weak, and degraded, and rapidly tending to extinction; when we observe, that the most authentic facts, respecting the present improved condition of the Cherokees and Choctaws, are utterly disregarded by nearly all those who urge their removal; and that the imagined interest of several States is constantly and powerfully at work to devise the means of acquiring the lands of the Indians;—and when we advert to the fact, that the President of the United States, and the Secretary of War, have repeatedly declared to the Cherokees, Creeks, and Choctaws, that these tribes cannot be protected against the laws of Georgia, Alabama, and Mississippi, although it is perfectly obvious, from the treaties themselves, and the construction which has been given them, ever since the year 1785, that one principal object of all the treaties was the protection of the Indians from all intrusion of whites, either for purpose of settlement or jurisdiction: When we see all these things, and remember that, in the language of Mr. Wilberforce, "Self-interest is an overmatch for benevolence," we cannot but feel greatly concerned, lest the character of our country should receive a deep and lasting wound, and the Cherokees and other tribes should experience great injustice.

There has never been an occasion, since the Declaration of Independence, on which it more became the People of the United States to speak their minds, than on the present. Every citizen who is capable of feeling any thing, must feel deeply for the honor of his country; every citizen ought, therefore, to become sufficiently acquainted with the merits of this question to express his opinion upon it.

Yet there is danger that the voice of the public will not be raised to such a note of earnestness and remonstrance as to arrest the present course of events. Certainly no one should presume that this will be done, unless men of character and intelligence in every part of our country will spend some time, and take some pains, to direct the attention of their fellow citizens to this subject.

But if the people generally, should manifest a deep interest in the pending controversy, and should insist on the most scrupulous regard to good faith, and to a kind, humane, and generous as well as just course of conduct with the Indians, it is plain that results highly beneficial may be expected.

The public conscience should be kept awake and alive to all public measures which are to have a bearing on the reputation of the country, or on the esteem in which the cardinal virtues of truth and justice are held. In regard to no subject whatever would a general apathy be so dangerous in its consequences, and so discreditable to the people.

In accordance with the views of the meeting which we represent, permit us to suggest, that meetings should be called in the various towns of the Commonwealth, where they have not already been held, at which meetings the *Rights of the Indians* should be considered, the preceding Memorial read, and measures taken to express the opinions and feelings of the people, in a memorial to Congress, from inhabitants of each town.

It is desirable that this should be done without delay, as Congress will probably act upon the subject at the present session; and within a few weeks public-spirited efforts in behalf of the Indians may be too late.

WILLIAM B. CALHOUN,   LEVERETT SALTONSTALL,
RUFUS CHOATE,   SAMUEL HOAR,
SAMUEL M. WORCESTER,   CHARLES G. LORING,
EDWARD REYNOLDS.

Deacidified using the Bookkeeper process.
Neutralizing agent: Magnesium Oxide
Treatment Date: March 2010

PreservationTechnologies
A WORLD LEADER IN COLLECTIONS PRESERVATION

www.ingramcontent.com/pod-product-compliance
Lightning Source LLC
LaVergne TN
LVHW011116210726
843642LV00016B/163